FRIENDS
OF ACPL

How the Doctor Knows You're Fine

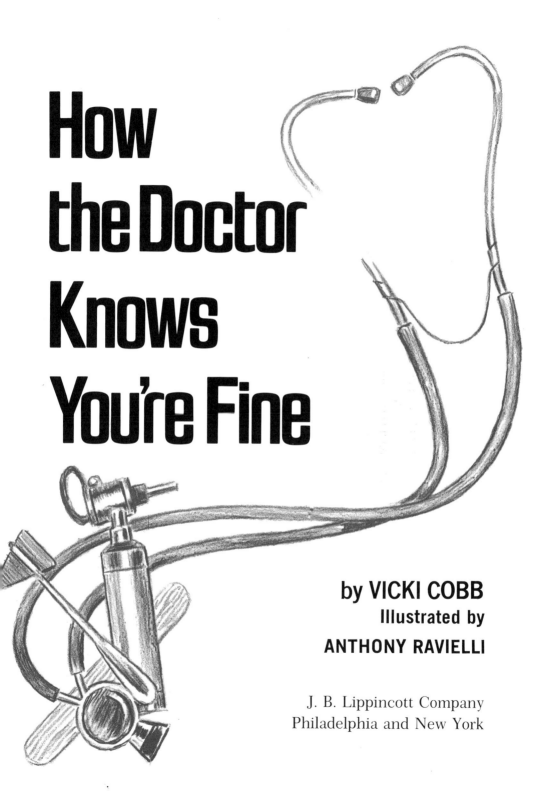

by **VICKI COBB**
Illustrated by
ANTHONY RAVIELLI

J. B. Lippincott Company
Philadelphia and New York

Dedicated to
Amy Rachel Zabb

Text Copyright © 1973 by Vicki Cobb
Illustrations Copyright © 1973 by Anthony Ravielli
Printed in the United States of America
First Edition

The author gratefully acknowledges the technical
advice of Ruth E. Kessler, M.D., F.A.A.P.

U.S. Library of Congress Cataloging in Publication Data

Cobb, Vicki.
   How the doctor knows you're fine.

   SUMMARY: Explains what happens during a physical examination
by the doctor.
   1. Children – Preparation for medical care – Juvenile literature.
[1. Medical care] I. Ravielli, Anthony, illus. II. Title.
R130.5.C6   616.07'5   73-4758
ISBN-0-397-31240-7 (reinforced bdg.)

How Are You Today?

Feeling fine! You know what feeling fine is like. It's feeling powerful enough to touch the ceiling. It's being hungry enough for seconds and thirds. When you feel fine you don't just walk to get places. You skip or run or jump or hop. You balance along ledges. You squeeze through gates and splash through puddles. Sometimes you get so you can't stop laughing. When you feel fine, every part of you, from your top to your toenails, feels super. Not one thing hurts.

But you will have days when you don't feel so fine. You know how it is. Sometimes your stomach hurts. Sometimes your head feels stuffed and one sneeze comes after another. Sometimes you have a scrape or cut that smarts and stings. On such days you don't feel much like running or jumping or even smiling. All you want is a warm, quiet corner at home. Love and care help too.

Aches and pains are no fun. Agreed. But they have an important job to do. Aches and pains say to you, "Stop! Hold everything! There is something wrong in your body and you had better do something about it!" Suppose you broke your leg and it didn't hurt. You might keep right on walking on it and then it would never get better. A doctor puts a cast around a broken bone so it can rest and heal like new. When you are sick, you feel like being quiet. Being quiet gives your body a chance to use all your energy to get you well. If you act as if you are fine when you are not, you can get sicker. Aches and pains are warnings that you should give your body a chance to get well again.

Do You Have to Wait

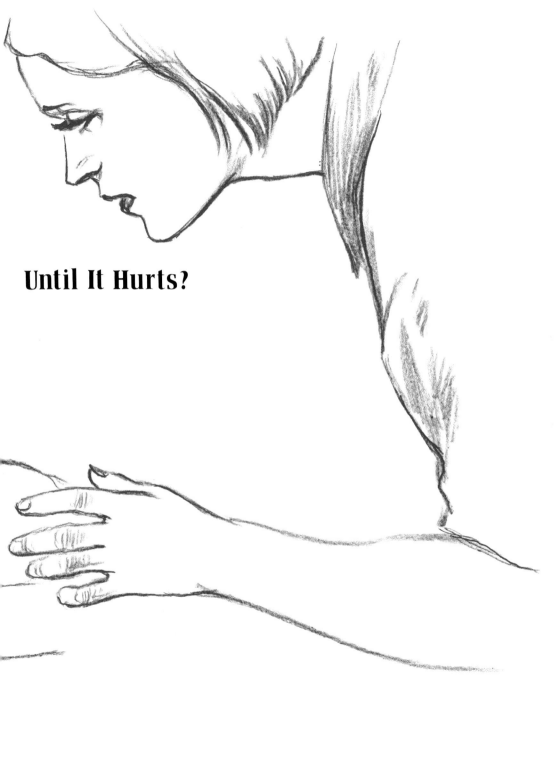

Until It Hurts?

Every day you do things that keep you well. You eat good food and get enough sleep. You brush your teeth and keep your body clean. Being clean keeps germs that might make you sick from collecting on different parts of your body. You also learn safety rules about crossing streets and using scissors and playing carefully so you don't get hurt. Taking care of yourself becomes a habit you don't have to think about. But when you think about it, habits that keep you healthy make a lot of sense.

One of the most important things you can do to keep well is to make regular visits to a doctor for a checkup. Doctors have ways of telling when you might get sick, before your body gives any pain signals. Doctors also give you shots and other kinds of medicine so you won't get certain sicknesses that children used to have long ago. A checkup gives you, your parents, and your doctor another way of knowing that you are in good health.

When a doctor gives a checkup, he or she is

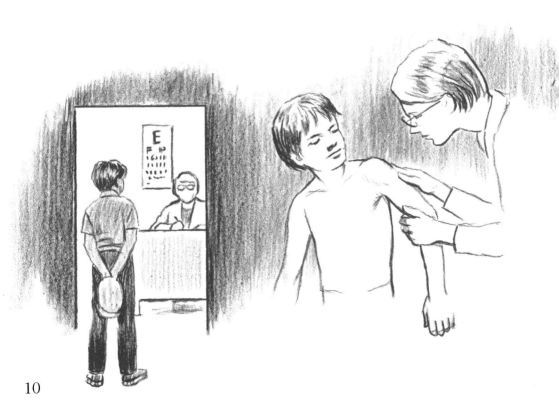

looking for early signs of trouble that could get worse and make you ill. If something is wrong, the doctor can treat it *before* it gets so bad it hurts. The kinds of things doctors look for are often not easy to see. Many early signs of sickness are so small they might not be noticed. Others are inside your body. All the things a doctor does to you during a checkup are special ways of knowing that your body is as well as it can be. You, too, can know how the doctor knows.

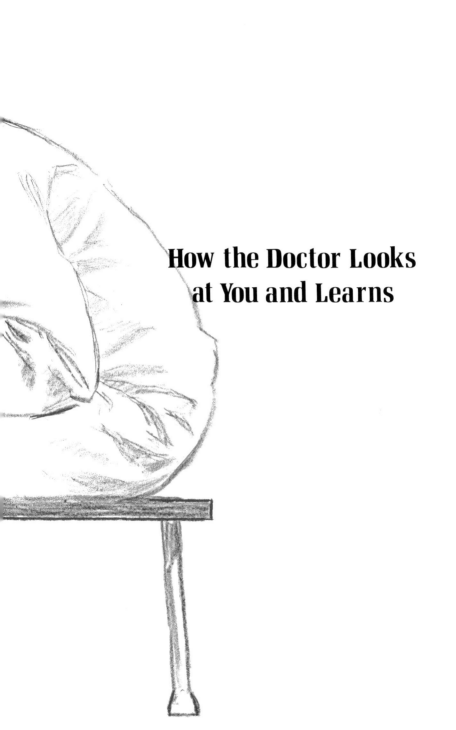

How the Doctor Looks
at You and Learns

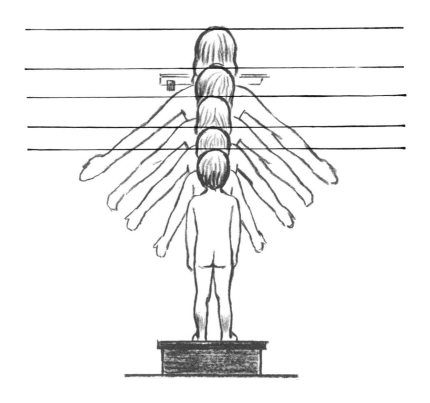

The first thing a doctor wants is a good look at your outside. So you get undressed. Then you are weighed and measured. The doctor writes down how heavy and how tall you are. She or he compares your weight and height with the measurements made at your last checkup. This is a way of knowing how much you have grown. Healthy children grow all the time. If you have grown, your doctor has a sign

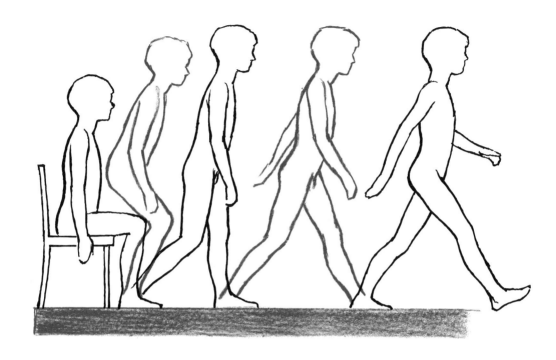

that you have been pretty healthy since your last checkup.

The doctor will ask you to stand and sit and walk. It's important to make these motions just as you always do. This is to see if your back is straight and if you walk properly. Some children have flat feet or walk with toes pointing in or out. If your walk is not perfect, the doctor may ask you to get special shoes or give you exercises to help you walk correctly.

Your skin can also help a doctor know that you are healthy. When you are well, the skin under your fingernails is a rosy pink. When you are not feeling well, this skin may not be as pink. If you have any rashes or sores the doctor takes a close look and may give you some medicine to make them clear up faster. Many children have small bumps on their hands or feet called warts. Warts are not serious but the doctor may want to help get rid of them, especially if they are in a place where they bother you such as the bottom of your foot.

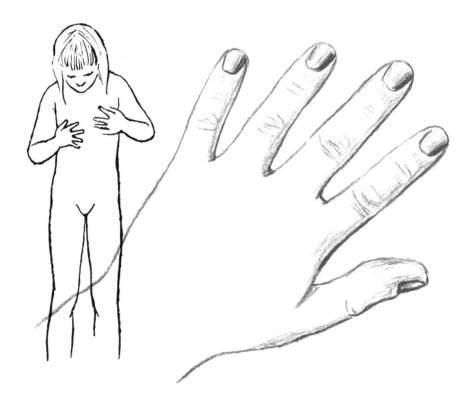

The doctor will examine your genital area. For boys, this means the penis and testicles. For girls, this means the vulva. Your doctor wants to see that your sex organs are clean and that there are no swellings or lumps that should not be there.

Windows to Your Insides

Your mouth, two eyes, two ears, and the two nostrils in your nose add up to seven openings in your head. These openings are like windows that allow your doctor to peek at what is going on inside you. Doctors use special instruments to see inside these openings.

One of these instruments is called an *otoscope*. It's a small, strong flashlight with a magnifying glass. The otoscope is used to look inside the small holes of your ears and nose.

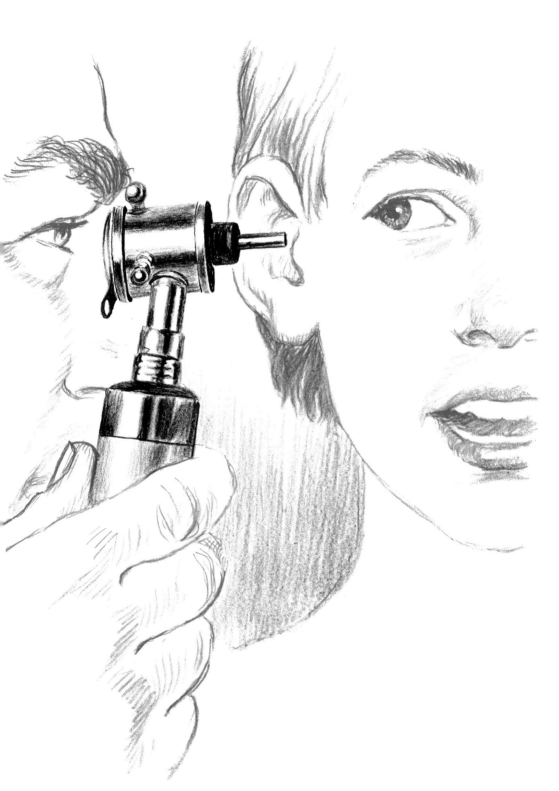

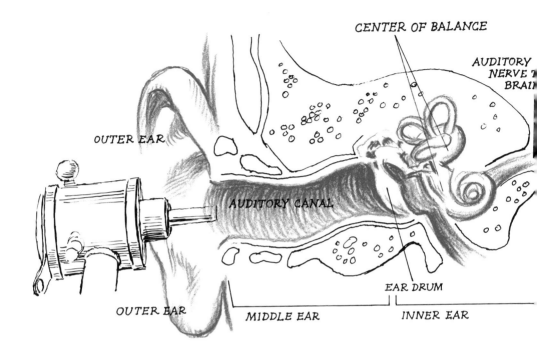

CENTER OF BALANCE

AUDITORY
NERVE
BRAIN

OUTER EAR

AUDITORY CANAL

EAR DRUM

OUTER EAR   MIDDLE EAR   INNER EAR

The parts of your ears that are most important for hearing are *inside* your head. They are
at the end of a tube of air called a canal. The
beginning of the ear canal is the opening your
doctor looks into with an otoscope. He or she
makes sure that your canal has the right shape
and that there is no redness or swelling. The
walls of the canal may have some brownish
wax that helps to protect the canal from disease-causing germs.

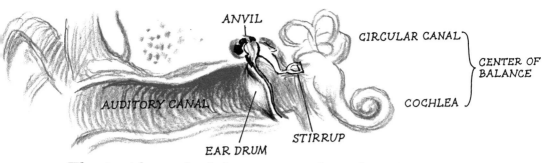

ANVIL

CIRCULAR CANAL

CENTER OF BALANCE

AUDITORY CANAL

COCHLEA

STIRRUP

EAR DRUM

The inside end of the ear canal is closed by a thin piece of skin called the *ear drum*. A healthy ear drum looks gray because not much blood goes through it. (Blood makes skin look pink.) It reflects a shiny cone of light from the otoscope and it's thin enough to show a bump where a tiny bone attaches to the unseen side of the drum. If you have an ear infection, the ear drum will not be as shiny and will be too thick for the doctor to see where the bone attaches.

The doctor also uses the otoscope to look inside your nostrils. Again it is to make sure there is no swelling, which would make it hard to breathe, and to see that your nose isn't running. If you get nosebleeds, the doctor checks to see where the blood comes from.

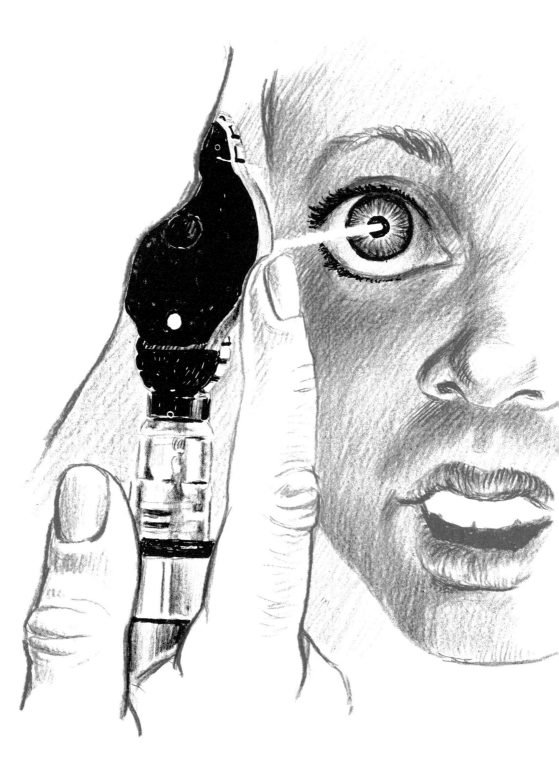

Another instrument, called an *ophthalmo-scope*, is used to look deep into your eyes. The hole the doctor looks into is the black spot or *pupil* in the center of your eye. The opthalmo-scope shines a light through the pupil that goes through the clear, jelly-like stuff filling the eye-ball and lights up the back part of the eye or *retina*. The retina is the one place in your body where a doctor can see very clearly the tubes or *blood vessels* that carry your blood. Many sick-nesses can change the way your blood vessels look, and these changes can be seen on your retinas. So if your retina looks like this picture, the doctor has another sign that you are fine.

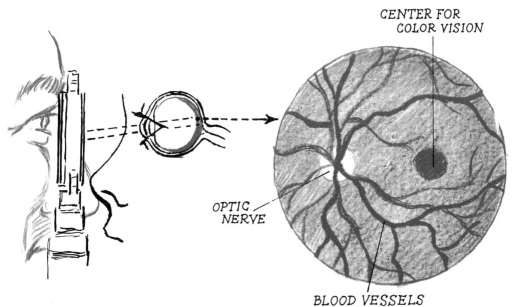

CENTER FOR
COLOR VISION

OPTIC
NERVE

BLOOD VESSELS

Germs that cause sore throats and colds can get into your body through your mouth. It's important for your doctor to get a good look at the back of your throat. You can help. Practice opening your mouth as wide as you can while saying, "Ahhhhhhhh." Use a mirror to see if you can see the back of your throat. The doctor may want to use a flat stick to press down the back of your tongue, but if you help, this may not be necessary.

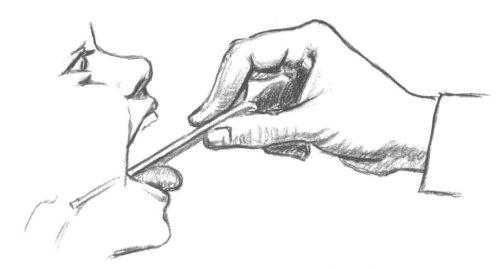

There is a lump called a *tonsil* on each side of your throat. Tonsils help to fight germs. In some people, the tonsils have fought so many germs they have become larger than normal and get sore very easily. If your tonsils are not too large and there is no redness, the doctor knows your throat is fine.

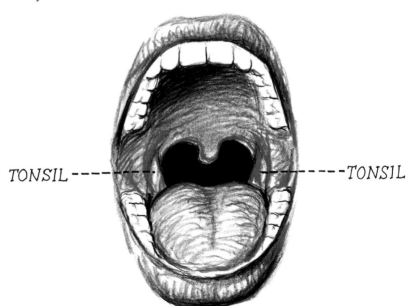

TONSIL --------- ---------TONSIL

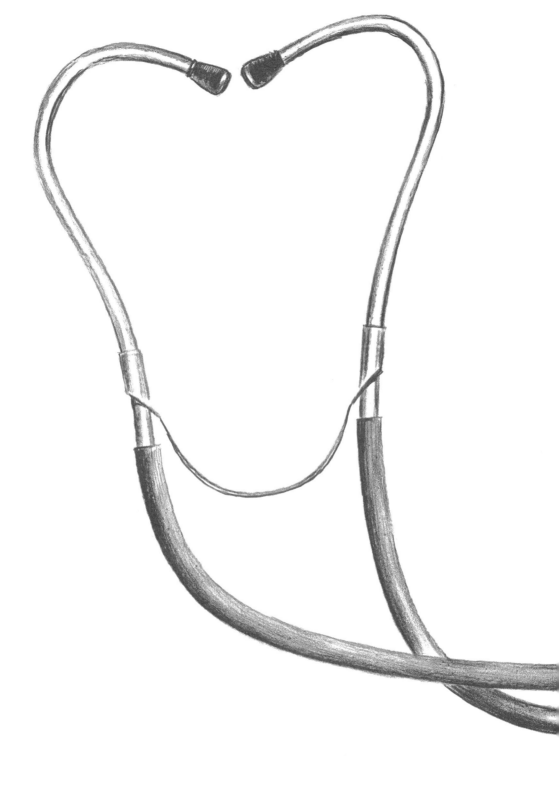

How the Doctor Listens
to You and Learns

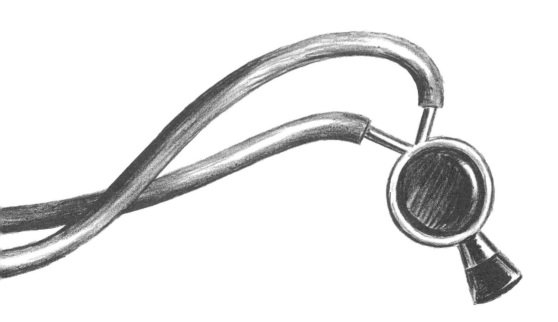

There are sounds inside your body that are clues to how two of your most important organs, your heart and lungs, are working. You can hear these sounds if you put your ear against someone else's chest. The doctor doesn't have to do this because of a special instrument called a *stethoscope.* A stethoscope is like a microphone for heart and lung sounds.

Your heart is a large muscle that pumps your blood around your body. It does this work by getting larger and smaller with a regular beat. A heart beat sounds something like, "Lub dub, lub dub." If the doctor hears any other sounds, something may be wrong.

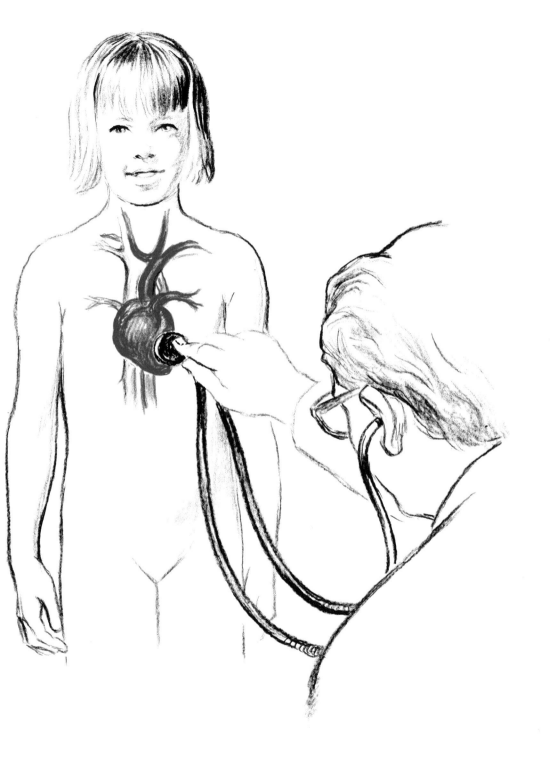

The doctor puts the stethoscope on your back to listen to the sound of air going in and out of your lungs as you breathe. If you have had a cough, the doctor hears a sound like a rattle when you breathe quietly. If your lungs are clear of any sickness, all that can be heard is "Swish, swish."

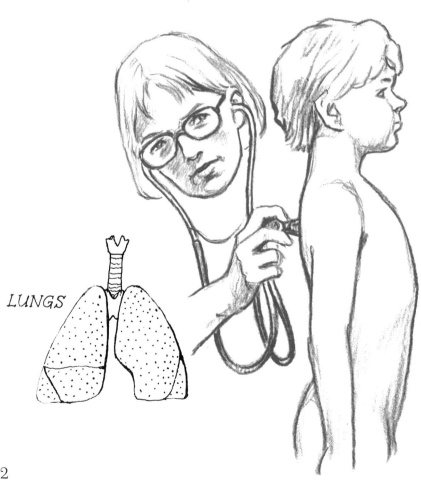

LUNGS

One of the most important ways a doctor listens to you is when you talk about how you feel. Don't hide anything. Be sure to answer your doctor's questions completely. If anything hurts be sure to tell him or her about it. The things you say about how you feel help a doctor know if anything is wrong, and help him or her to know how to get you well if there is something wrong.

Your doctor can also find out how well you see by listening to you. You may be asked to read aloud the letters on an eye chart. Each line of letters is smaller than the line above and, of course, is harder to see. You will be asked to cover one eye and read the chart with the other. If you don't make any mistakes with the small letters, your doctor can be sure that you don't need glasses and your vision is fine.

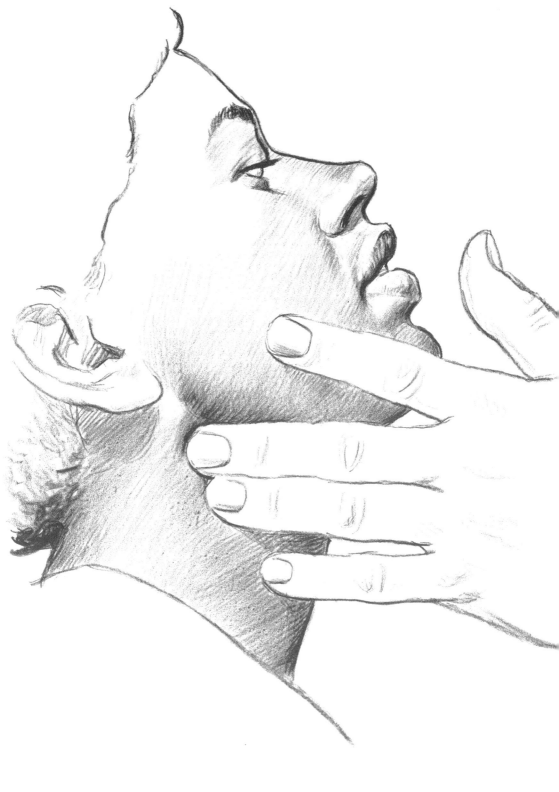

How the Doctor Touches You and Learns
You and Learns

A doctor's hands are also special instruments for finding out if you are all right. Doctors have learned how to touch the soft part of people's bodies under the ribs. By pressing gently, your doctor can feel the hard edges of your liver, which has the job of removing things from your blood that may harm you. If your liver has been working too hard at this job, it may get larger and become tender. So your doctor makes sure that it is not larger than it should be. These gentle presses should not hurt at all, but if there is any pain be sure to say something about it.

The doctor bends your elbows and knees to make sure they move easily in the right directions. She or he uses a small hammer with a rubber head to test your reflexes. A reflex is a movement you don't have to think about making in response to a touch. The doctor gently taps your knees with the hammer and watches how your legs move. Your doctor also taps the backs of your heels and watches the movements of your feet. Normal reflexes are another way of knowing everything is fine.

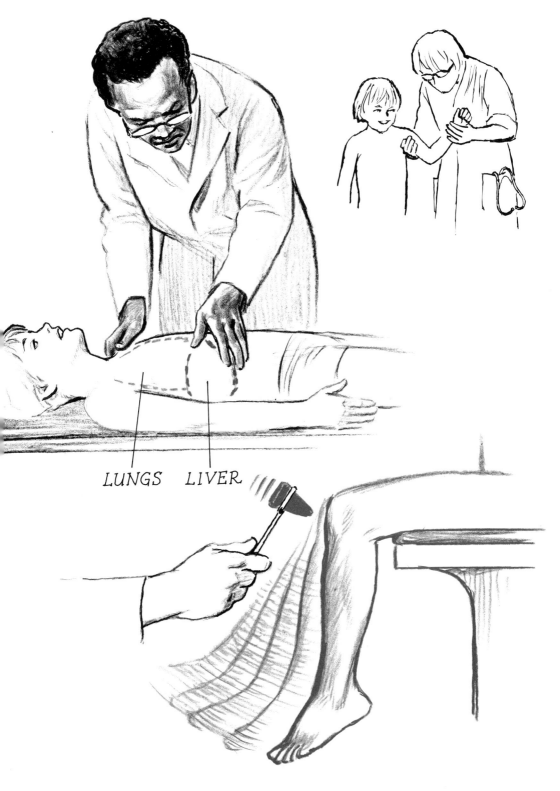

LUNGS   LIVER

There are small glands, like tonsils, in your neck and armpits that sometimes swell when you are ill. The doctor feels these glands to make sure they are not swollen or tender.

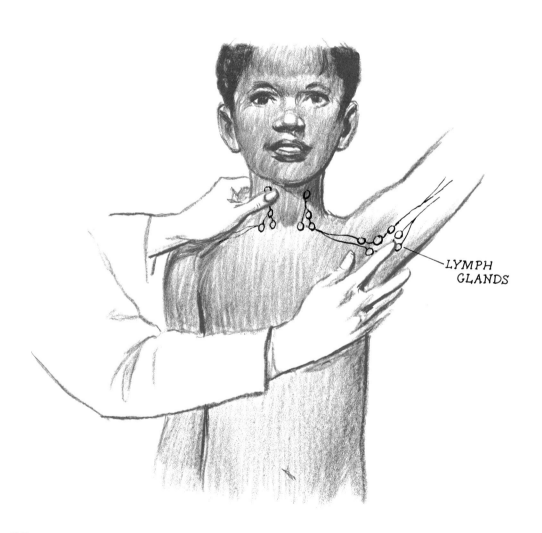

LYMPH GLANDS

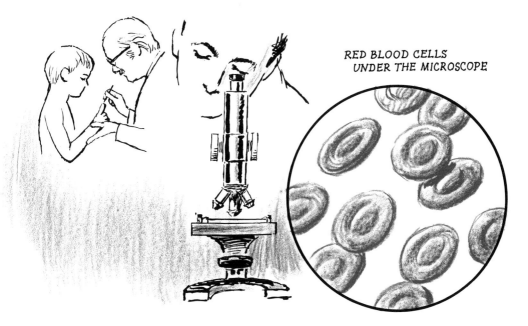

RED BLOOD CELLS
UNDER THE MICROSCOPE

Your blood also contains many signs that show how healthy you are. Blood does many jobs. One is to carry oxygen to all parts of your body. Another is to help fight germs. A doctor can tell if your blood is doing these jobs by seeing how red it is and looking at a drop of blood under a microscope. In order to get some of your blood, the doctor will have to make a small prick on your finger or arm. This may hurt a little but the amount a doctor can learn from a look at your blood is more than worth a tiny bit of pain. Besides, a prick on the finger hurts far less than the cuts and bruises you often get when playing.

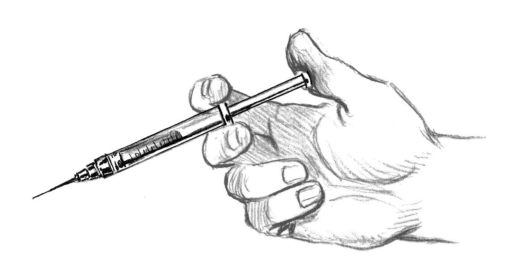

Why Get Shots?

Long ago many children got diseases that were very serious. Sometimes children died and other times an illness left them blind, or deaf, or unable to move a part of their body. There was only one good thing about getting one of these diseases for a child who was lucky enough to live through it. She or he could be certain of never getting it again. The blood of such a person would always carry a special material to fight the germs that caused the disease before sickness had a chance to ever start again.

Today there are special medicines called *vaccines* that make it impossible for you to become sick with these diseases. A vaccine contains the germs that cause a disease but these germs are very weak. Your body fights these weak germs as if they were the real thing. In this way your body makes what it needs to fight disease-causing germs and becomes like the body of a child who, long ago, lived through the disease. The only difference is that you are protected from the disease without actually having been sick.

Some vaccines are simply a good-tasting sip of syrup. But most have to be injected into your body with a needle. This hurts a little, but it hurts less if you relax and let the doctor do it quickly. It helps to think how lucky you are. Instead of weeks of a terrible illness, all you ever feel is a tiny prick in your skin.

Helping Nature to Help You

The main job of protecting you from sickness and helping you to get well is done by your body. Your skin keeps most germs from getting inside you. Sometimes a few germs will get past your skin through a cut or through your mouth or nose. When this happens your blood rushes to the rescue. Redness and swelling are caused by extra blood that comes to fight germs. If germs get past this extra blood into your entire body, you may get a fever that can also kill germs.

Long ago, before doctors knew what they know today, each person's body had to fight sickness all by itself. But today doctors can help. They can give you medicine that helps to kill germs faster than your body can do it alone. Doctors can also give you medicine that will make you feel more comfortable while your body does the fighting. Often, a doctor can give you medicine that will kill germs before they have a chance to spread through your whole body and make you really sick. This is why doctors take special care of cuts and why checkups are important. If you take care of yourself when you are well, your body is a stronger fighter for the times when you get sick.

When you are healthy it's easy to forget what it's like to be sick. A checkup twice a year lets you know that you have been doing the right things to take care of yourself and it reminds you to keep up the good work. A healthy body is a must if you want to enjoy being alive.

Index